IT'S THE END OF THE WORLD!

SOLAR STORM

BY ALLAN MOREY

BELLWETHER MEDIA • MINNEAPOLIS, MN

TM

Are you ready to take it to the extreme? Torque books thrust you into the action-packed world of sports, vehicles, mystery, and adventure. These books may include dirt, smoke, fire, and chilling tales. **WARNING**: read at your own risk.

This edition first published in 2020 by Bellwether Media, Inc.

No part of this publication may be reproduced in whole or in part without written permission of the publisher.
For information regarding permission, write to Bellwether Media, Inc.,
Attention: Permissions Department,
6012 Blue Circle Drive, Minnetonka, MN 55343.

Library of Congress Cataloging-in-Publication Data

Names: Morey, Allan, author.
Title: Solar Storm / by Allan Morey.
Description: Minneapolis, MN : Bellwether Media, Inc., [2020] | Series:
    Torque: It's the End of the World! | Audience: Ages 7-12. | Audience:
    Grades 3 to 7. | Includes bibliographical references and index.
Identifiers: LCCN 2019000944 (print) | LCCN 2019002383 (ebook) |
    ISBN 9781618916556 (ebook) | ISBN 9781644870846
    (hardcover : alk. paper)
Subjects: LCSH: Coronal mass ejections–Juvenile literature. |
    Electromagnetic pulse–Juvenile literature. | Solar activity–Juvenile
    literature. | Electric power failures–Juvenile literature. |
    Sun–Corona–Juvenile literature.
Classification: LCC QB529 (ebook) | LCC QB529 .M67 2020 (print) |
    DDC 523.7/5–dc23
LC record available at https://lccn.loc.gov/2019000944

Text copyright © 2020 by Bellwether Media, Inc. TORQUE and associated
logos are trademarks and/or registered trademarks of Bellwether Media, Inc.
SCHOLASTIC, CHILDREN'S PRESS, and associated logos are trademarks and/or
registered trademarks of Scholastic Inc., 557 Broadway, New York, NY 10012.

Editor: Rebecca Sabelko   Designer: Andrea Schneider

Printed in the United States of America, North Mankato, MN.

TABLE OF CONTENTS

BLACKOUT!

You watch colorful streams of light fill the night sky. The beautiful **auroras** mean that danger is near. Magnetic **energy** is washing over the planet.

Sparks begin to fly from electrical wires. Then the power goes out. You are plunged into darkness. A solar storm just caused a worldwide **blackout**!

BRIGHT LIGHTS

The aurora borealis is a brilliant light show. It is seen at night in northern parts of the world. It is created by electrically charged particles in the atmosphere.

AURORAS

You do not just lose power.
There is no phone service. Nothing
electrical works!

The power outage stretches for
days. Without electricity, stores close.
Banks shut down. You start to worry
about how you will get food. Without
power, food in the fridge quickly
spoils. Soon your family will run out
of supplies.

7

A CME REACHES EARTH!

A solar storm is caused by a huge release of energy from the Sun. A **coronal mass ejection**, or CME, is then shot into space. As it hits Earth, **satellites** stop working. TV and phone services are interrupted. The **Global Positioning System** gets knocked out.

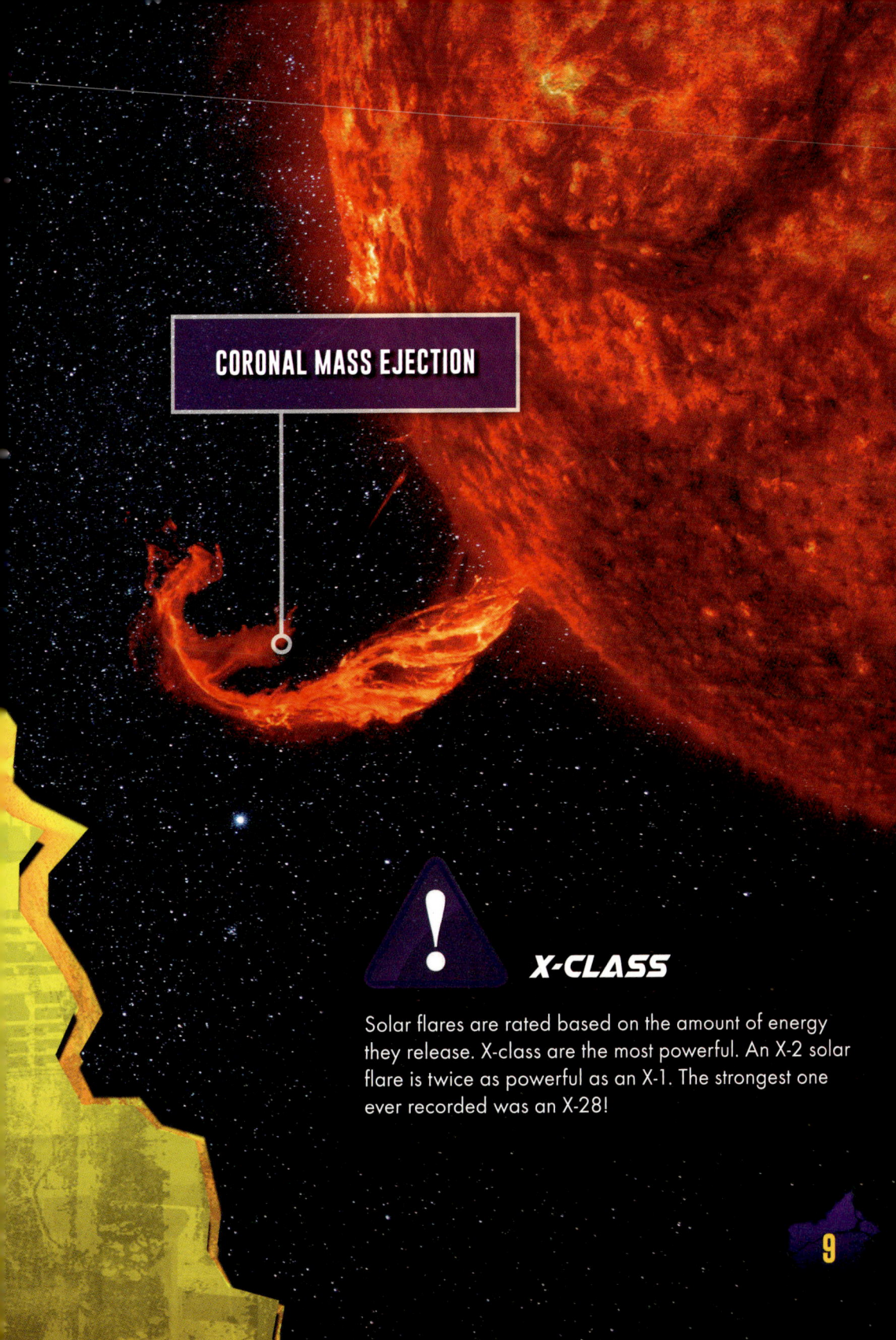

CORONAL MASS EJECTION

X-CLASS

Solar flares are rated based on the amount of energy they release. X-class are the most powerful. An X-2 solar flare is twice as powerful as an X-1. The strongest one ever recorded was an X-28!

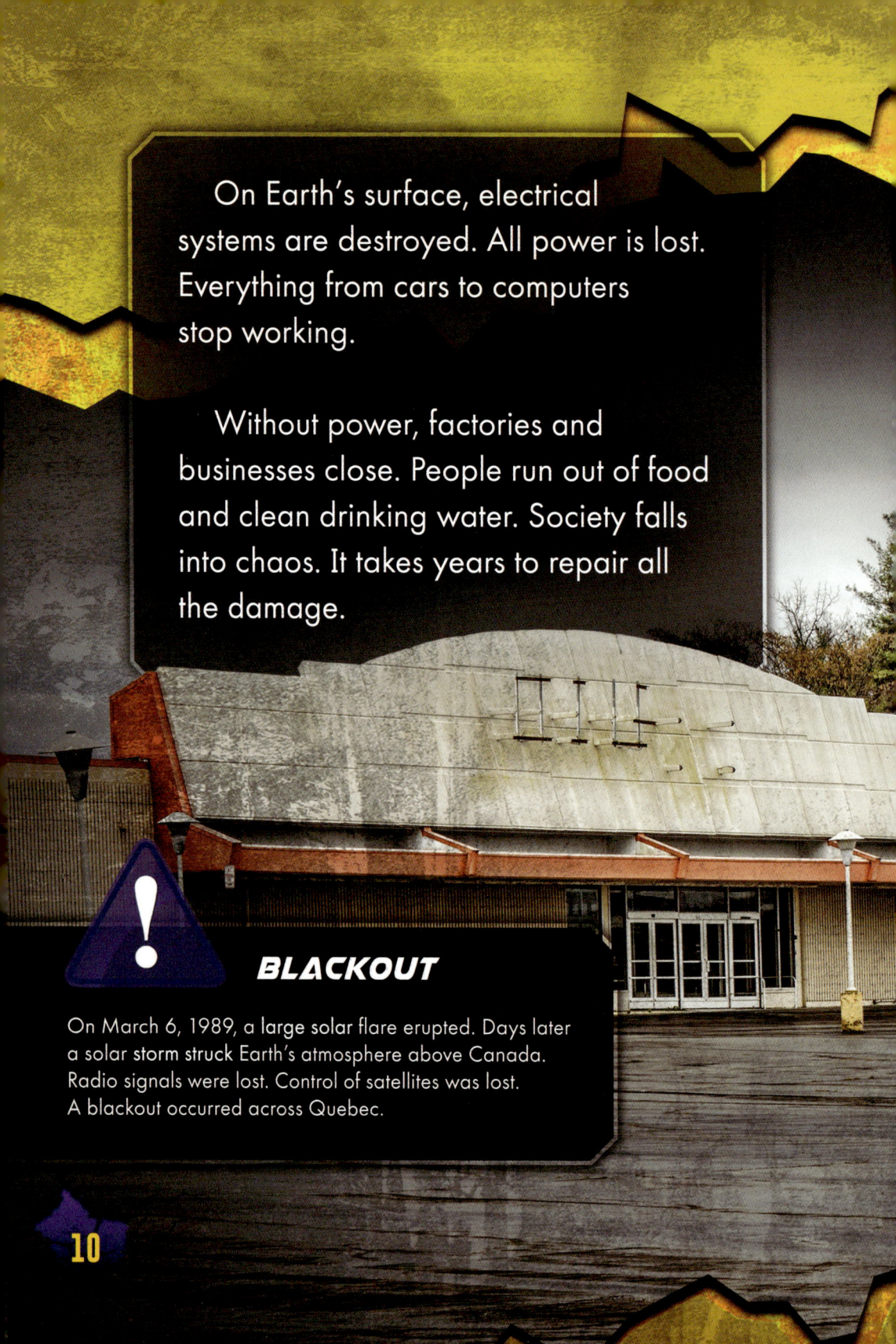

On Earth's surface, electrical systems are destroyed. All power is lost. Everything from cars to computers stop working.

Without power, factories and businesses close. People run out of food and clean drinking water. Society falls into chaos. It takes years to repair all the damage.

BLACKOUT

On March 6, 1989, a large solar flare erupted. Days later a solar storm struck Earth's atmosphere above Canada. Radio signals were lost. Control of satellites was lost. A blackout occurred across Quebec.

CHAIN REACTION

solar flares erupt on the Sun

hours to days later, a CME reaches Earth

satellites and electronics stop working

there is a worldwide blackout

society plunges into chaos as food supplies run out

HOW WOULD A SOLAR STORM HAPPEN?

The Sun is a **violent** place. Explosions constantly boil up on its surface. They create **solar flares**. These are huge bursts of energy. The power of a solar flare is equal to millions of **nuclear bombs**. Powerful solar flares can affect **radio signals** here on Earth.

Large solar flares shoot clouds of **plasma** into outer space. Most of the time, these CMEs are not on course with Earth.

PLASMA CLOUDS

A LOOK BACK:
THE CARRINGTON EVENT

SEPTEMBER 1859

RICHARD CARRINGTON

Richard Carrington recorded a large solar flare. Within a day, a huge CME washed over the northern hemisphere. At the time, electricity was not widely used. But it was needed to send messages through telegraph wires. Messages could not be sent.

But when Earth lies in the path of a CME, a solar storm occurs. It causes amazing auroras. Satellites **orbiting** Earth may be damaged or destroyed. Blackouts can happen. There is little that can be done to prevent damage.

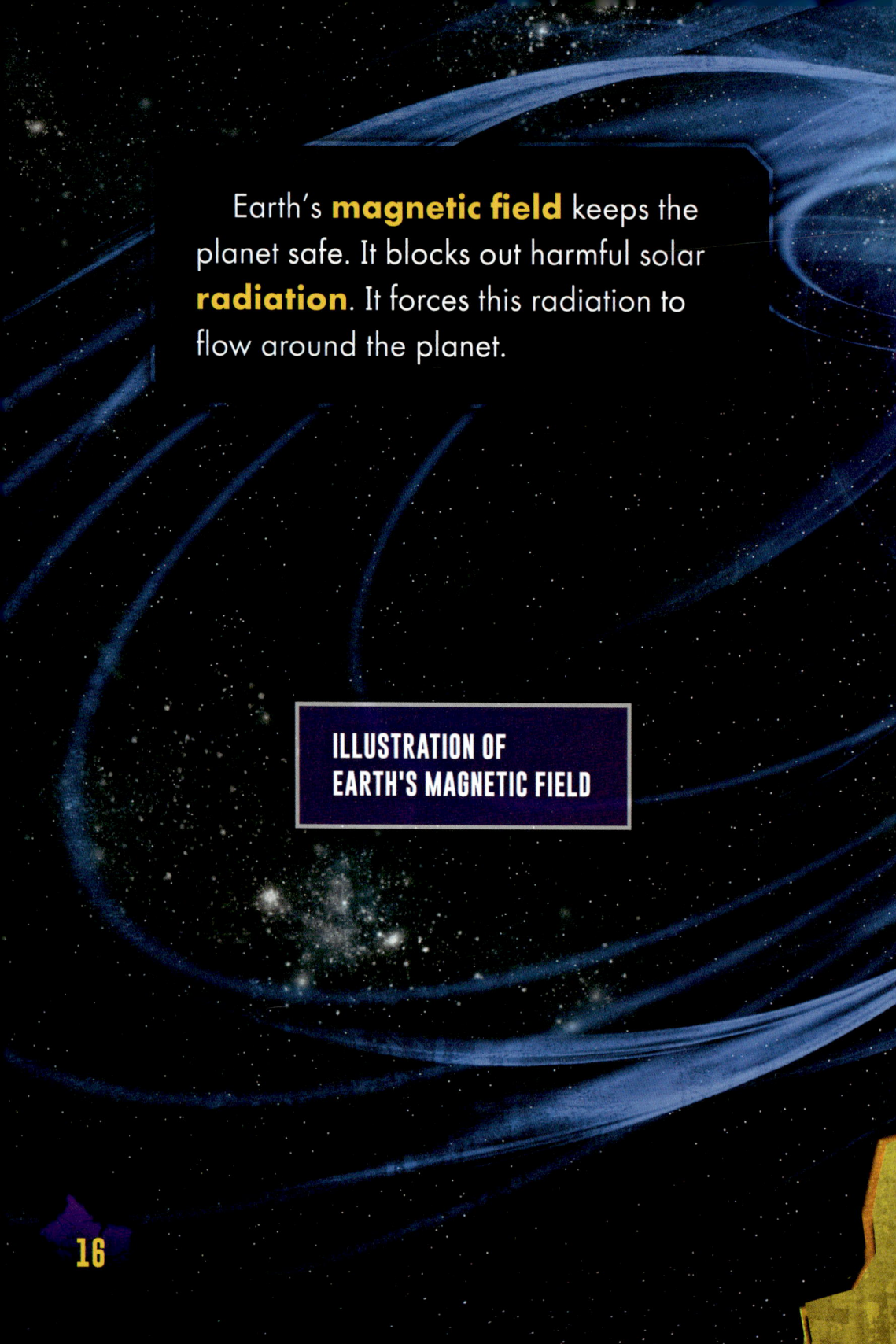

Earth's **magnetic field** keeps the planet safe. It blocks out harmful solar **radiation**. It forces this radiation to flow around the planet.

ILLUSTRATION OF EARTH'S MAGNETIC FIELD

CME

But the energy from a powerful CME can break through the magnetic field. It can cause electrical interruptions. Widespread power outages happen on Earth.

HOW LIKELY IS A SOLAR STORM?

Solar storms have occurred in the past. They will continue to happen.

The Sun goes through a cycle every 11 years. Scientists believe the next cycle has already started. They also think it will be a very active one. This means that more solar flares might erupt on the Sun's surface.

A MATTER OF TIME

During active years, more than 1,000 solar flares can erupt. Most present no danger. But every few years, a huge solar flare erupts on the Sun. It is only a matter of time before one of these sends out a CME that hits Earth.

ILLUSTRATION OF
NASA SATELLITE

Scientists are not sure what causes solar flares. But they are learning how to **predict** the causes of solar storms. **NASA** satellites observe the Sun. They keep track of spots on the Sun. They record activity on the Sun's surface. Predicting solar storms will help protect the planet!

GLOSSARY

auroras—natural events that cause streaks of light to appear in the sky, most often near Earth's poles

blackout—a period of darkness caused by power failure

coronal mass ejection—an event that causes large amounts of charged particles to shoot from the Sun into space; CMEs can disturb radios and other electronics on Earth.

energy—usable power that comes from heat, electricity, or other sources

Global Position System—a system using satellites that allows people to know their exact position on Earth

magnetic field—an invisible energy field that surrounds Earth

NASA—National Aeronautics and Space Administration; this U.S. agency is responsible for space exploration.

nuclear bombs—the most dangerous weapons on Earth

orbiting—moving around something in a fixed path

plasma—a gaseous group of charged particles

predict—to guess when something will happen

radiation—a type of dangerous and powerful energy that is released by the Sun

radio signals—invisible energy waves used for communications

satellites—objects that orbit planets

solar flares—sudden bursts of energy on the Sun's surface

violent—using powerful forces in a destructive way

TO LEARN MORE

AT THE LIBRARY

Dickmann, Nancy. *Exploring the Sun*. New York, N.Y.: Rosen Publishing's Rosen Central, 2016.

Koehler, Max. *Journey to the Sun*. New York, N.Y.: Powerkids Press, 2015.

Rathburn, Betsy. *The Sun*. Minneapolis, Minn.: Bellwether Media, 2019.

ON THE WEB

FACTSURFER

Factsurfer.com gives you a safe, fun way to find more information.

1. Go to www.factsurfer.com
2. Enter "solar storm" into the search box and click 🔍.
3. Select your book cover to see a list of related web sites.

INDEX

The images in this book are reproduced through the courtesy of: T photography, front cover (before city); kdshutterman, front cover, pp. 2-3, 20-21 (after city); Markus Gann, front cover, pp. 20-21 (Sun); Iuliia Lukova, pp. 4-5 (buildings); biletskiy, pp. 4-5 (auroras); aslysun, pp. 6-7 (girl); Grappler, pp. 6-7 (city); cgterminal, pp. 6-7 (auroras); NASA Goddard/ NASA Images, pp. 8-9, 11 (top right), 17 (CME inset), 19 (satellite inset); Carolyn Frank, pp. 10-11; Skorzewiak, p. 11 (top left); Andrey Armyagov, p. 11 (middle left); RJZA, p. 11 (middle right); Migel, p. 11 (middle bottom); solarseven, pp. 12-13; Color 4260, pp. 14-15; Wiki Commons, p. 15 (Richard Carrington inset); Marc Ward, pp. 16-17 (magnetic field); Triff, pp. 16-17 (Earth); Jurik Peter, pp. 18-19.